Summary: PRINCIPLES

Life & Work

by Ray Dalio

EXECUTIVE**GROWTH**
S U M M A R I E S

For those who dare ask more, learn more and become more.

Table of Contents

BACKGROUND

Ray Dalio went from being an ordinary middle-class kid from Long Island to one of the 100 wealthiest people in the world. Along the way, he developed some meaningful relationships, changed his perspective, and discovered one or two secrets about running a successful company and living a great life.

His company, Bridgewater Associates, started in his two-bedroom apartment, and has gone on to become the world's most successful hedge-fund, now managing roughly $160 billion. This was only possible because Ray learned to handle mistakes and think about "not knowing."

Everyone with goals and dreams can learn from this book. The principles in it offer a radically different approach to the way most businesses operate, how they make decisions, and how they treat their employees. On the other hand, there is something excitingly logical and straightforward about all of them.

The Principles outlined in this book are distilled from years of experience, and the author believes that they can be applied by anybody to achieve success. He doesn't believe that his success was due to any single remarkable thing about him. Rather, it came from his determination to put these ideas into practice, find out the truth about each mistake he made, and learn through the process.

There are two major sections. The first one examines Life Principles in depth, and the sub-points are numbered to refer back to the original text. Within this section you will also find "**Lessons in Action**" where we interweave dense, theoretical advice with relatable stories. The second section examines how these principles translate into the language of business.

"I hope that these Principles will help you visualize your own audacious goals, navigate through your painful mistakes, have quality reflections, and come up with good principles of your own that you will systematically follow to produce outcomes that vastly exceed your expectations."

POWER INSIGHTS

As our valued reader, we cherish your time and focus. When reading the following **Power Insights** you will instantly capture the key learning points of *Principles*, create an effective mental map of the book, and be able to better retain the remainder of the summary.

***

Highly successful entrepreneurs tend to be independent thinkers, and they don't easily give up on their goals, no matter how audacious those goals might seem to everyone else.

This has certainly been true of Ray Dalio, the author of this book who is also one of the most successful businessmen and is in the top 100 wealthiest people (according to *Forbes*) in the world. Over the span of 40 years, he has deliberately and systematically cultivated a highly effective mindset in his personal life. Along the way, he has shaped Bridgewater, his multi-billion dollar hedge fund company, using the same set of **Principles**.

What are these Principles? To quote Dalio:

"Principles are fundamental truths that serve as the foundations for behavior that gets you what you want out of life."

In life, the same kinds of things tend to happen over and over again. If you can learn to elevate your thinking, start to see these recurring patterns of events, and translate those patterns into principles of your own, you will eventually have a template for dealing with just about anything that life throws your way. In this way, you systematically cut out the guesswork and continuously make better decisions. Dalio's approach is grounded in common sense and logic, along with the tough lessons won from hard experiences.

The first Life Principle is to embrace reality and to deal with it well. A lot of people fail at this because they insist on wishing that life was different in some way, or they mistakenly believe that their version of "reality" is the only correct one. As a result, their habitual behavior and their work are ineffective.

Success can only come from working effectively with reality, and from learning how to deal with not knowing. Failure should never be seen as a personal insult, but rather, as a useful tool to improving your methodology and honing your skills.

As painful as it is to fail, you can use those failures to set up **feedback loops for rapid learning**. Then you can mine those failures for wisdom that will enhance your understanding of all the complexities of reality, as it relates to your specific sphere of business or life.

It takes courage to hold yourself and other people accountable, but there's no point in avoiding reality. Don't allow your feelings about failure to undermine your success – face the totality of the situation and keep failing bravely until you master the underlying principle. Personal evolution only happens when you understand that **pain combined with proper reflection is a recipe for progress**.

The second Life Principle is in the form of a Five-Step Process. You can use this process to tackle any challenge, overcoming it in order to achieve what you want out of life.

1) **Make sure that your goal is clear**. Human beings have needs and desires on many levels, so it's important to take the time to think clearly about exactly what it is that you're going after and why you're going to invest the time and effort to get it. Aim high, and aim for something that will enhance your life in the long run.

2) **Clearly identify the problems that stand in the way, and don't tolerate them**. Never allow the hassle, pain, or drudgery of dealing with problems get the best of you. Embrace the process and don't allow negative emotions to cloud your higher reasoning.

3) **Diagnose the Root Cause of the problem**. It's easy to confuse causes and effects and miss the root of the problem. Don't waste time constantly addressing symptoms – dig deep into the details to find the Principles involved, and always be thorough.

4) **Design a Plan**. Begin with an outline and then drill down into the details, one by one. Refine your plan as you go along to keep it aligned with reality.

5) **Push through to Completion**. No matter what. If you don't have the self-discipline, enlist the help of someone else who has the characteristics you lack.

The third Life Principle is perhaps the most important of all: **Be Radically Open-Minded**. In Dalio's view, the two most troublesome obstacles in life are self-generated, and we all suffer from them to some degree. These two obstacles are **your ego and your blind spots**.

If you convince yourself that you know it all and remain closed off to the ways others see things, you're going to struggle a lot more in life. Merely arguing for the sake of arguing, or insisting on being right, can easily make you blind to the subtleties of each situation – the ones that make all the difference. That's why it's so important to acknowledge these two weaknesses, and to learn to deal with them effectively by becoming radically open-minded. It's the unique ethos that underpins all of Bridgewater's success.

The fourth Principle: Understand that People are Wired Differently. Some of us are great at creative problem solving but aren't too sharp at taking care of each and every little detail. Meanwhile, others excel at the details. Dealing with these differences among people in an open and honest way fosters success. Ignore them at your own peril.

The human brain is an amazing piece of equipment, and when you begin to understand how it's wired, you can also learn how to get the most out of it. For example, the Amygdala is a brain structure that regulates emotions like fear and anger. If you understand how it works and how it can hijack your reasoning abilities, you can learn how to work around it. Good intentions alone are never enough – hard science can help fill in the gaps.

The fifth and final Life Principle is all about Learning How to Make Decisions Effectively. In this chapter, the author explains how he has approached all the major decisions in his life and business. He has learned to **navigate the different levels** of any issue at hand and learned how to **synthesize**. Effective synthesis means collecting masses of data and forming it into an accurate picture that reflects reality as accurately as possible, then visualizing all the possible outcomes.

Reality is always complex, and there are always endless possible ways that the future could play out. Some eventualities are more probable than others – and the key is to know whose opinion is the most **believable**. Intuition helps, but logic combined with the best information available is more important. Dalio has refined a number of revolutionary computerized "decision-making algorithms" to help him synthesize as effectively as possible, both for investing and for the logic that runs his company.

The final part of the book shows how these five principles can be applied to the challenges of running a successful business. The idea is to align the values and the evolution of the company to the values and the personal development of the individuals that work there.

Bridgewater employees are expected to embrace **Radical Truth and Transparency.** Employees make decisions by **weighing the believability** and the merits of each idea. "Idea Meritocracy" is a progressive philosophy compared to the usual autocratic way of running a business. It's a company culture that insists that everyone has the right to know and to think for themselves, rather than just follow instructions blindly.

Idea Meritocracy needs to be based on trust. The foundation for this culture rests on meaningful, open, and honest relationships. Everyone needs to uphold the idea that loyalty to the common mission is more important than loyalty to individual people. **It's okay to make mistakes, but it's unacceptable not to learn from those mistakes**.

Backbiting, company politics, and divisive behaviors are like cancers to any organization. Dalio believes that it is **only when people are in sync with each other** that they can be open-minded and assertive at the same time. The ideal climate for progress comes about when everyone agrees that weighing the believability of an idea, rather than its popularity, leads to the best decision.

There are always going to be disagreements, so learn how to get beyond them quickly. Idea Meritocracy only works when it is grounded in clear, solid, and tested procedures, and when those procedures are always open for everyone to evaluate and refine.

When you look down on your business **the way an engineer looks down on a machine**, you're able to **constantly test and evaluate** it, to make sure it's giving you what it is designed to do. You're able to align people who are wired in certain ways to their job functions without being swayed by sentimentality, prejudice, or ignorance.

When the "machine" breaks down, you can **diagnose the root causes** and **design improvements** to get around the problems.

For Idea Meritocracy to work in practice, people need to:

1) Feel that they are allowed to put their honest thoughts on the table;
2) Feel comfortable about having thoughtful disagreements with each other, and;
3) Have clear procedures to get past disagreements.

As a 64 year-old veteran of financial and personal development, Dalio wants to share these ideas freely with people because they have been so instrumental in forging his own path. He firmly believes that following these principles will help you to combine your passion with your work. They're tools to help you struggle well, and to help you evolve as a person.

"It's up to you to decide what you want to get out of life and what you want to give."

***

If you enjoyed the **Power Insights** and want to keep a copy as a reference or to share with your friends and family members, feel free to download your exclusive digital copy by scanning below.

Follow the steps below to instantly access your exclusive Power Insights PDF Guide:

1) **Open** your smart phone's camera application

2) **Aim** your phone's camera **and focus on** the QR Code below

3) **Click** the link that pops up on the top side of your screen

Or by following this link in your browser:

https://www.exegrowth.com/pdfguide-plw-37

Now get ready to uncover the principles of success that very few hold. See you on the other side.

PART I:
WHERE RAY DALIO IS
COMING FROM

"We are all born with different thinking abilities but we aren't born with decision-making skills. We learn them from our encounters with reality."

Where Ray Dalio Is Coming From

Ray's success in life didn't come from what he knew. Rather, it came from knowing how to deal with *not knowing*. Over the course of his life, he learned to make every decision, in both his personal life and his business life, based on a set of **principles** that helped him cut through the confusion and succeed.

These principles help him know what's true, and they help him identify what to do about it. Ray made a lot of mistakes in his life, and he is willing to admit that they have been painful mistakes. However, reflecting on those mistakes has helped him to create his life principles, maximize his odds of his being right, and given him a healthy fear of being wrong. They've become part of him over the years.

Ray has always been an independent entrepreneurial thinker with audacious goals, and he has always had a hunger for a deep, universal understanding of the workings of reality. **His life's work has been to systematize this understanding into a set of fundamental truths**. He is now at the stage of his life (68 years old at the time of writing) where he wants to share this knowledge with others.

His fundamental principle can be summed up as follows: Think for yourself in an open-minded and clear-headed way and make up your own mind about *what you want* and *what is true*. Now decide how to achieve what you want in light of what is true.

Our encounters with reality serve to hone our decision-making skills – that has been his approach all along.

Ray used this system of thinking to overcome his weaknesses and maximize his strengths. For example, he has a bad rote memory and didn't like school. He rebelled against things he didn't want to do, but pushed ferociously for the ones he took an interest in.

He first became interested in stock trading around the age of 12 while he worked as a caddy at a local golf course called Links. His first investment was buying $5 shares of Northeast Airlines. He ordered all the annual reports from *Fortune* magazine in 1966, and worked his way through each and every one of them. While in high school, Ray was a successful young entrepreneur and the stock market was still booming, but he was unprepared for what was to come.

The years between 1967 and 1979 provided a pair of terrible economic surprises that led to major losses and some painful lessons. These developments instilled an urgent need in Ray to understand macro-economic laws as thoroughly as he could.

During college, he majored in finance, which helped set the foundation. Later, when he was inspired by the Beatles in India, he also learned to meditate, which helped him develop an invaluable, calm open-mindedness. That was all during the era of free love, mind-expanding drug experimentation, and youth rebellion against the establishment. In 1971, Ray graduated with a nearly perfect grade point average and enrolled in Harvard Business School.

That same year, the global monetary system was in meltdown. He spent that summer researching world financial collapses, and he began to see patterns of cause and effect. He worked at a brokerage and handled his own accounts on the side, starting his company, Bridgewater.

One of the biggest lessons he learned was that there are no safe bets in trading. A "can't lose" trade ended up costing him $100,000, devastating him financially. That pain completely changed his approach to decision-making and spurred him on to create his principles and to record them.

Ray began to see pain as a reminder that he still needed to learn more. It became like an elegant game, and the more he played, the better he got at the game and the less pain he had to endure. By now, he had achieved and surpassed all of his goals. More importantly, he had discovered his chief source of satisfaction: **The art of struggling well.**

Making money was never his primary goal. Instead, he wanted a mission in life, and he wanted meaningful relationships with inspiring people. The money was merely a bonus, and there were times when he was flat out broke.

After eight years in business, Ray was regularly writing his *Daily Observations,* which are still widely read by business leaders. Ray's experience in the livestock, meat, grain, and oilseed markets allowed him to formulate his first set of rules and principles for understanding market volatility. McDonald's used his theories to make a lot of money when they introduced chicken McNuggets.

Meanwhile, Bridgewater was successful in many other ways. Paul Coleman joined Bridgewater, and the two of them ran the company in a seat-of-the-pants sort of way from Ray's brownstone home, where he lived with his wife, Barbara, and their two sons. Paul and Ray became a great match because of the way they challenged one another openly and honestly. Inside Ray's brownstone is where many of his principles evolved.

The economy was in terrible shape between 1979 and 1981. For their little company, these years were like a series of blows to the head with a baseball bat. Ray made certain economic predictions in the *Daily Observations* that turned out to be dead wrong. It was humiliating, and very public – and the business suffered. At one point, he had to let go of all the Bridgewater employees, one by one. It was a gut-wrenching time, but it provided a huge lesson in how to balance his aggressiveness and how to perfect his timing.

But it was also a blessing in disguise. In the process, he learned to be radically open-minded and to accept the fact that he didn't know everything. He got to work creating a system that minimizes risk while maximizing profitability – and he started putting all the principles he was learning into writing. He analyzed the economic and inter-personal machinery to identify recurring patterns: "Another one of those."

Along the way, he perfected his computerized "Holy Grail" method of stock trading. Computers simply make better decisions than people do, provided you take into account the proper constraints and conditions.

Bridgewater went on to become the top-performing U.S. bond manager in the world. That brought new challenges – including the challenge of how to manage staff members in a growing organization. That challenge led to the idea of decision-making with 'idea meritocracy,' and led Ray to learn about shapers, neuroscience, and what drives people. He learned to match people's merits to their jobs.

During the final phase of the "hero's journey" of his life, and looking back from a higher level, Ray can see how his perspective has changed. Now he's sharing his principles with you so that you can evolve and learn to struggle well too.

"My most fundamental work principle: Make your passion and your work one and the same and do it with people you want to be with."

PART II:
LIFE PRINCIPLES

"In order to have the best life possible, you have to:
1) Know what the best decisions are and
2) Have the courage to make them."

1: Embrace Reality and Deal with It

Lessons in Action: Introduction

Mary-Elizabeth is a talented and hard-working artist and paints the most incredible portraits in a style reminiscent of the Dutch Masters, but she's also a hopeless idealist. Living reclusively and avoiding contact with the outside world, she spends countless hours behind the canvas, perfecting her skills, but subconsciously avoiding reality.

Jess comes over one evening, the two of them get into a bottle of wine, and the conversation starts flowing. Soon they're in a deep discussion.

"If only things were different. In a perfect world, artists would be like movie stars," Says Mary-Elizabeth.

Jess laughs at her friend encouragingly. "Don't think that way," she says, "you're super-talented! You'll figure it out."

"I don't know why people don't buy my art. If I don't sell anything soon, I won't make the rent."

"It's that bad, huh?" Jess asks, as lines of concern appear on her brow. She puts her hand on her friend's shoulder.

"I don't belong in this world." Mary-Elizabeth's eyes grow dark, and a scowl covers her face as she speaks. "People just don't appreciate real art anymore. There's no place for artists anymore."

"Well, it's the world we live in – and it's not all that bad." Jess tries to speak soothingly. It might just be the wine, but clearly her friend is on the verge of tears.

Mary-Elizabeth shakes her head. "This 'real world' you're talking about is cruel, fake, and soul-less."

Jess knows better than to disagree with her friend when she's in this kind of mood. Instead, she invites her along for a weekend getaway near the lake. Maybe a change of scenery will change her state of mind.

*

Ray Dalio's first principle is all about the state of mind you choose to develop, which translates into the way you approach *reality*. **You can either try to avoid the harsh realities of life or you can face them openly and honestly for what they are (1.1, 1.2).**

Each person will decide how hard they're prepared to work, and what they will sacrifice in order to be able to either savor life or make an impact on the world. Those two extremes needn't be mutually exclusive either. Each person has to figure out the truth on their own – and the best way to fast-track that process is to be **radically open-minded and radically transparent (1.3).**

Avoiding reality is counter-productive. Constantly avoiding or disguising your own weaknesses will never allow you to transcend them. Being completely open and transparent gives you the freedom to truly be yourself and simultaneously opens the channels of understanding between you and other people.

It's painful at first, but it is truly liberating in the long run. You become free from the burden of self-deceit, doubt, and the fear of not being good enough in the eyes of others. Once you've mastered it, **you no longer see failure as a personal insult.**

Success is not really a matter of working harder, but rather, it's about working more effectively in line with reality. Ray's approach has been to see each new problem as a puzzle, and by solving it, he unearths a gem in the form of a principle, which can then be applied to similar problems: "Another one of those".

This sets up a feedback loop that leads to rapid learning, which is often painful, but also provides a kind of high. That high eventually becomes a new habit because it's addictive. There's nothing more rewarding than growing as a person. It has been the key to Ray's success, and it's what he is referring to when he talks about "learning to struggle well."

If your focus is only on how you appear to others (as either "good" or "bad," or as "successful" or "a failure") rather than on achieving your goal, you're actually avoiding reality and playing ego-games. **Honest feedback from reliable people** is invaluable. It accelerates learning and helps you understand others as well.

Nature provides beautiful lessons on how to go about it (1.4). We can become fixated on first-order consequences and forget about the second- and third-order consequences. Evolution means constant change, and it cares nothing for any individual's ideas about "good" or "bad." The balance is always in favor of benefiting the whole. **Evolving becomes life's reward (1.5).**

Looking at nature from a top-down perspective (1.10), you discover harmonious laws that drive ecosystems. The same view helps you understand economics, politics, and human history. Looking from a bottom-up perspective gives you a different understanding. You get to see how universal laws translate into specific environments. Both points of view are necessary to understand nature and live successfully.

Natural things adapt (1.6), the strong survive, and DNA holds onto the winning formula when individual creatures die. Their successes are passed on to new generations. Holistically, as a system, progress is guaranteed.

Knowledge serves the same purpose for individual human beings, nations, and organizations or companies. We can learn about what works and what doesn't by knowing what others have tried before and by examining their logic – even though they're long gone.

By aligning your individual incentives with what's good for the whole, you progress. The satisfaction comes from your individual evolution – not only from the monetary success. **Pain plus reflection equals progress (1.7).**

If your behavior is aimed only at avoiding pain, you won't progress (1.8). If you learn to manage that pain and allow the process to teach you (by reflecting on the principle it contains), you will be successful. That means **holding yourself and others accountable (1.9)** instead of avoiding responsibility or being unrealistically jaded about your failures.

*

Lessons in Action: Application

The weekend away turns out to be exactly the right medicine for Mary-Elizabeth. The first day she complains about the bugs and the blisters on her feet, but by the second day, the magic of nature starts smoothing out the creases, and by the time the sun has set, she's smiling again and feeling more like herself.

"I'm sorry I've been such a pain." She eventually says to her friends, who are all sitting by the edge of the lake, watching the sunset.

"Well, I'm glad you're getting back to your old self." Laughs Jess, "It's good to see you smile again. It's been a while."

"I know. I've been so stuck in my head and brooding too much. Just look at how incredible all of this is." She opens her arms wide, as if to embrace the sublime natural scene in front of them. "I do belong here." She sighs.

That night, she starts talking to Adrian, who was also invited along for the weekend by Jess. He has recently started an online business, creating professional web profiles for achievers. He's full of enthusiasm, and it's contagious. They hit it off and end up talking for hours.

As they chat, it feels to Mary-Elizabeth as if something is opening up in her mind. It's as if her horizons are stretching wide, and as if a fog is lifting. Adrian comes up with the idea to offer her portraits into the deal for his clients – he'd been looking for a suitable artist anyway.

"It would be great to capture something about their core values in an artistic way," he says. "I think some of the guys I'm targeting will love the idea. Can you digitize your work?" Mary-Elizabeth is about to object, but she catches herself in the act and changes her mind.

"I'm sure I can find out how to do it." She says instead.

In the weeks to follow, her friends watch the changes start to unfold in her. In just three weeks, Adrian manages to secure a couple of commissions for her, leading to a new kind of dynamic energy about her art.

Although Mary-Elizabeth still prefers oil on canvas to digital art, she has found a way to compromise with the kind of world she's really living in. It takes months to pick up the new skills she needs – and there is still a long way to go – but challenging as it is, she's learning to adapt to the world in new ways and keeps building on her success.

> *"I have found it helpful to think of my life as if it were a game in which each problem I face [reality] is a puzzle I need to solve. By solving the puzzle, I get a gem in the form of a principle that helps me avoid the same sort of problem in the future. Collecting these gems continually improves my decision making, so I am able to ascend to higher and higher levels of play"*

2: Use the 5-Step Process to Get What You Want Out of Life

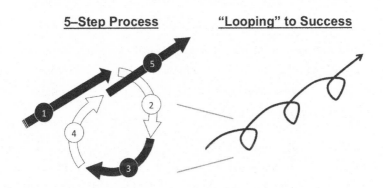

5–Step Process

"Looping" to Success

Step 1: Have Clear Goals

Everyone has goals and desires, but **not everyone is clear about their goals**, and fewer still achieve all of their goals. Sometimes it's hard to decide what to aim for – because there are so many things that we want to pursue.

Sometimes our goals are sensible, but they go against what we desire to do. You might have the goal of being physically fit, but you might not like to exercise or you're unwilling to change what you enjoy eating, for example. **It's important to reconcile your goals and your desires.**

The best goals are those that will enhance your life in the long run, and the ones that make sense in the widest possible perspective. Even seemingly unattainable goals can be achieved, because as you progress, your ideas about what is possible keep expanding. If you remain flexible and remember that failure isn't personal, there's no reason you can't improve your life.

Think clearly, prioritize your goals, and be audacious enough to aim high.

Step 2: Identify the problems, and don't tolerate them

Nobody achieves ambitious goals without solving some tough problems along the way. The difference between people who succeed and people who fail rests in the way different people approach those problems.

Some people avoid facing their recurring problems at all costs **because they're unpleasant or painful**. They don't believe the problem can be solved. Others fail to identify the real problems while they fight imaginary ones instead, or they confuse the root cause of the problem with the symptoms.

That's why it's important to be precise and clear-headed when identifying the root cause. Make sure you know what problems are big and what ones are small. Focus your time and energy on one big, central problem at a time, and that will solve many smaller, incidental ones. Never allow a problem of any kind to derail your progress. Don't sweep them under the rug and hope they'll disappear. Instead, develop a severe intolerance for them.

Step 3: Diagnose the Root Cause

Digging down into the details of what's causing the problem takes time and thorough analysis. Most of us jump instantly to proposed solutions – but that often doesn't work. Once you scratch off the veneer, there is often an underlying root cause that's tricky to solve.

Missing a train, for example, is a proximate cause, while the real cause of the fault is forgetfulness.

Quite often, people miss the correct diagnosis because they're afraid to objectively judge the abilities, talents, and natures of other people. It's even more difficult to be objective about your own failings. But this is a vital part of the process.

Step 4: Design a plan

For this step, you'll need to call on your higher-level thinking and look down on your path from the proper perspective. From this elevated vantage point, you can visualize the problems, potential outcomes, and possible routes to your goal. It's like visualizing the storyline of a movie.

The best way to start is by first sketching out your plan in the broadest possible outline and then systematically drilling down into the details. Major goals are split into smaller, more manageable ones, and then into specific tasks that are measurable.

Write it down, systematize it, and track your progress against your plan. When the need arises, re-evaluate and fine-tune your planning.

Step 5: Push through to completion

This step requires the most personal discipline. It helps to see how each individual task relates to your overall goal in order to keep your motivation up. Tick off each item on your to-do list, one by one, and persevere.

If you're terrible at sticking to self-imposed to-do lists, it can be useful to forge a symbiotic relationship with another person who is good at it. They can help to keep you focused and disciplined, even if you're no good at it yourself.

Take each step on its own and complete each one before moving to the next. Impatiently jumping from goal-setting to problem-solving confuses things in your mind. Few people will excel at all five steps, and each of us has weaknesses. But that doesn't matter in the slightest.

Unearthing those weaknesses leads to personal growth, and being honest and humble about them allows you to find the best way around them. Combining humility with mental-mapping (knowing what to do) is a recipe for success.

"It seems to me that the personal evolutionary process takes place in five distinct steps. If you can do those five things well, you will almost certainly be successful...together, these five steps make up a loop..."

3: Be Radically Open-Minded

Lessons in Action: Introduction

The Big Argument, as it would later be called, had reached a screaming crescendo, and if little Robbie hadn't blown that camping whistle at the back of the bus and forced dad to pull over, there might have been a tragic accident, and at least one divorce.

The entire extended McKenzie family was packed into Granddad's old bus on their way back from the farm when all hell broke loose. The argument had been simmering for weeks. At issue was the decision of whether or not to move most of the family out of the city, back to the farm, and go off grid. Almost everyone agreed it was a good idea, but almost everyone had a strong opinion as to how to go about it. Nobody could agree, and dad, who was behind the wheel, was the most emotional of everyone.

There were far more questions than answers, but everyone thought they knew best. As The Big Argument developed into a raging schism, it was really about ego and not about practicalities. Nobody was willing to look at the big picture, and nobody was prepared to give up their point of view.

The McKenzies were a close-knit family, and most of them were forward-thinking. This big decision, however, threatened to tear the family apart. In the end, it was Aunt Sarah, the quiet one, who convinced everyone that there was a better way to approach the decisions that needed to be made.

*

Ray Dalio believes that this is the most important chapter in his book, and that it contains the secret to overcoming **your two biggest obstacles in life: Your ego and your blind spots (3.1)**.

The ego barrier, as it is defined here, is the lower subconscious part of your brain (the amygdala) that interferes with your higher brain function (the logical and conscious prefrontal cortex) by bringing up your deep-seated fears and needs. Our hardwired survival and acceptance drives are examples of these.

Everyone's brain is wired in basically the same way, but some people have found a way to transcend their self-division, whereas others have not. This is what makes all the difference.

When you get angry with yourself, it is a sign that your ego is wrestling with your higher self. When someone challenges your thinking, and you get angry with them, it's a sign that your ego feels threatened. **The need to appear knowledgeable, or to be right, is hijacking your pursuit of truth**. Even the most intelligent people suffer from it. It's helpful to become more aware of this process that is always at work within you.

Each one of us also has certain **blind spots**. We tend to view ourselves, and our place in the world, from fixed points of view. This makes us blind to other potential ways of seeing things. This is usually the fatal flaw that prevents us from living up to our full potential. Instead of harnessing different people's diverse ways of thinking (such as lateral thinking and logical thinking) to deal with problems effectively, we get stuck in an impasse, blind to our own shortcomings.

The way to get beyond these two major obstacles is through practicing Radical Open-Mindedness (3.2). It's human nature to want to be right and to appear right in the eyes of others.

People that make the best decisions are rarely convinced that they have all the answers. They are open-minded enough to recognize the value of multiple inputs, specifically multiple points of view from others who may know more than they do. They value learning, reading, and discovering new approaches. They understand that making the decision comes after gathering all the relevant facts. They have also developed a healthy fear of being wrong. Usually that comes from experience – from crashing and burning and going through the pain.

There's a big difference between arguing and seeking out the truth. Arguing is a war between egos, whereas searching for truth comes from a pure motive. Sometimes you're the teacher, but more often, you have to assume the role of the student. A wise person knows the difference.

Ray Dalio talks about **believability**. He defines a "believable" person as one who has a proven track record of turning their approach into success. On health matters, for example, it's likely that your doctor is more believable than you are. When you're the more believable person, it's useful to remind the other person of that fact in a tactful way, which is a big part of **the art of thoughtful disagreement (3.3)**.

If there is a disagreement, it's unlikely that both parties are right. It pays to figure out which one of you is wrong instead of blindly insisting on being right. To accomplish this, you need to approach each disagreement from a calm, openly curious state of mind, suspending your knee-jerk ego reactions as far as possible.

That takes practice. You need to learn to spend your time in productive discussions with believable people, rather than wasting it on arguments with small-minded egotists. There's no place for anger in this process. Another useful tactic is to **triangulate your point of view with the views of experts (3.4)**, while also getting those experts to disagree thoughtfully with each other. This way, you get a much wider view of complex issues, enabling you to make the best possible decision.

Our egos and our blind spots are primitive mental mechanisms that get in the way of open and honest exchanges of facts and lines of reasoning. Some of us are timid, and some of us are bombastic – but finding the truth should override differences in personality.

It takes time and effort to cultivate the art of radical open-mindedness (3.6), and it can be painful to let go of ideas that you're attached to. Instead of letting that pain prevent you from making the best possible decision, let it become your guide.

Cultivate the habit. When you feel frustration and pain, know that your amygdala is kicking in, and take a moment to calm yourself and open your mind before going any further. Each time you succeed, you become stronger and better at decision-making.

Ray practices transcendental meditation, and it has helped him develop his calm, even-minded temperament. For him, meditation eventually solidified into a permanent habit. It was not an inborn talent – he learned to do it, and so can you.

Over time, it becomes instinctive to make decisions based on facts and the best information available instead of from your own limited point of view. You gradually become radically open-minded.

*

Lessons in Action: Application

All the McKenzies were shocked when Aunt Sarah stood up on the table and told everyone to quiet down. Nobody had suspected that this shy little dormouse could command so much attention when she wanted to.

"You're all being pig-headed," she said, as she stared everyone down. "And it's getting us nowhere. If we're going to make this happen, we need to set aside our egos and our petty differences, and look at the big picture in a calm and systematic way."

There were murmurs and comments, but Granddad shut everyone up and told them to listen, threatening that they could walk home if they didn't. Aunt Sarah spoke for a long time, calmly, persuasively, and logically. She acknowledged that each family member had good ideas, but opinions weren't enough. There were facts to consider – and someone had go through the trouble to find out what those facts were.

In the end, it took more than five years to move the entire McKenzie clan off grid. There were plenty of obstacles and challenges on the journey, lots of changes, and many new things to learn. Along the way, there were bruised egos and hurt feelings, but something stronger than all of that helped keep them all together.

It was only because Aunt Sarah had shown everyone that finding the truth was more important than being right, that any of it was possible at all. Her calm open-mindedness had made it possible. She showed the rest of them how to have a thoughtful disagreement instead of an argument.

> *"Being radically truthful and radically transparent are probably the most difficult principles to internalize, because they are so different from what most people are used to."*

4: Understand That People Are Wired Very Differently

Lessons in Action: Introduction

Bob Prince worked with Ray Dalio, and the two of them were great intellectual sparring partners. When they attempted to systemize their global understanding of bond markets, however, their project hit a rough spot. Bob headed up the team, but the results were far from satisfactory.

They couldn't get the conceptual thinkers to work well with the more literal thinkers. Ray and Bob had to think about why their project was failing. The problem seemed to be that nobody knew what anybody else was good at, and that everyone had his or her own opinion. Everyone was pulling in a different direction and everyone was getting angry and frustrated.

They stuck to their guns and started figuring it out. It was painful, but what they learned was turned into a valuable Life Principle, and that's what this chapter is about.

*

The phenomenal success of Bridgewater as a company was not a matter of chance. It came about because the team, led by the maestro holding the baton, Ray Dalio, worked harmoniously in line with the Principles outlined in this book. Part of the secret came from understanding the realities of economics, but another important part came from **understanding the human brain.**

Research into neuroscience unlocked a vital principle: **People's brains are wired differently (4.1)**. If you take this into account when assigning roles and responsibilities, you're bound to be more successful than if you blindly ignore it.

For Dalio, the penny dropped when his own kids underwent **psychometric testing** and he learned painful lessons during his son's struggle with bipolar disorder. Intrigued by the insights these tests provided, he became determined to study the subject more thoroughly and apply what he learned in his growing company. His experience had already taught him the frustration of failing to get the right results from the wrong types of people.

Some parts of our brains and minds are "elastic," meaning that they can be changed to some extent. Other parts are impossible to change. **Knowing about these limitations and possibilities makes a big difference (4.2)**. You can't expect people who are wired one way to excel at a task that suits a different brain type. **It's far more sensible to give them a task that suits their unique abilities (4.3, 4.5)**.

Bridgewater employees underwent comprehensive testing to determine each of their unique individual inclinations and talents. The results were captured and displayed for all to see on **"Baseball Cards."** At first, there was resistance to the process, but these days, the company couldn't run without the cards.

Working with professionals and researchers from Harvard University, the Wharton School, and the University of Virginia, among others, Dalio spent years perfecting the process. It was **groundbreaking research into how companies can encourage the personal development of their employees**.

Evolution has formed the human brain over millions of years. We also share certain brain mechanisms with other animals. What makes us different is our proportionately larger neocortex – the wrinkled grey mass of brain matter responsible of learning, planning, imagination, and higher-level thought-processing. Our brains are uniquely capable of reading the intentions and mental states of other people. Most of what drives us is physiological, as two separate parts of your brain wiring are constantly fighting to control "you."

Many of our decisions are made by our subconscious minds, which can sabotage the plans of our higher, conscious reasoning. Animals are not divided this way. They follow instinct automatically. Humans are different, and it's hard to accept that there are large parts of our brains that simply aren't logical. Once you learn to see how these mechanisms operate in your own brain, and in the brains of others, you become far better at getting the results you want.

Feelings, for example, are regulated by our amygdala – a little almond shaped structure in the cerebrum. It happens mostly under the surface of our alert consciousness. **These feelings (like anger and fear) can hijack your higher reasoning – without your being aware of what's happening**. Successful people have learned to reflect on what triggers the hijack and have consistently found ways to work around it. They've learned to deliberately cultivate useful habits that support the goals of their "upper level" selves.

Habits control most of our behavior. When we're on "autopilot," the basal ganglia has taken over from the cortex in the brain. A lot of people constantly undermine their own success because of bad habits that they're not fully conscious of. **If you really want to change, the best way is to patiently and kindly train your automatic brain to enjoy habits that support your highest goals.**

Bridgewater used knowledge gained from neuroscience to create comprehensive tests to determine people's brain wiring and **find out what they are like (4.4)**. The basic categories are:

- **Creators** (Innovative and unconventional)
- **Advancers** (Carry out ideas effectively; understand the human brain)
- **Refiners** (Good at spotting flaws; love facts and theories)
- **Executors or Implementers** (Focused on details; gets things done)
- **Flexors** (Combine all the others; adapt well)

These are only the fundamentals, and most people have bits of each type in them, even if they lean more toward one category. For example, "creators" are seldom good at getting things done or taking care of each and every detail. Placing the right "brain type" in the right business function was one of the big secrets of the success of Ray Dalio and Bridgewater.

*

Lessons in Action: Application

After much research, the problem was revealed. Bob was not surrounding himself with the right type of people. He chose people who were "Flexors" like himself, and talented as they were, the results were disastrous.

Bridgewater began to use the new psychometric tools (like the baseball cards) they were developing to diagnose what was going wrong. After much deliberation, they decided to give Bob a new deputy, who excelled at "independent and systematic thinking" or an Advancer. She was a better match for Bob's particular brain type because she could take his big ideas and translate them into specific tasks with deadlines.

She, in turn, hired detail-oriented people (executors), including an effective project manager, to move the project out of deadlock and toward completion. With the new team, and individuals who were suited to their specific responsibilities, the bond systemization project started humming.

"While "know thyself" and "to thine own self be true" are fundamental tenets I had heard long before I began looking into the brain, I had no idea how to go about getting that knowledge or how to act on it until we made these discoveries about how people think differently."

5: Learn How to Make Decisions Effectively

Lessons in Action: Introduction

"How is this time going to be any different?" Meg was asking. Alistair had to admit, he didn't know, but he was sure that something needed to change. Neither one of them could go on this way anymore, but he knew there had to be a way forward, even if he couldn't see it at the moment.

"I'll be honest with you, baby," He said as calmly as he could, *"I'm not sure how, but I am sure we can do it. We just have to get better at making decisions and carrying them through."*

"I'm sick and tired of working all the time and never getting anywhere." Meg flung the dishcloth into the basin in frustration. *"I just can't see what's going to change!"*

"I know," Alistair sighed, *"Me too. I'm burning out."*

"You've been flipping from one construction job to the next, but you'll never make enough that way to build our house like we always said. And I can't stand the jobs I'm stuck doing." Meg looked desperate, and tired to the bone. *"We've been winging it for three years now, and we're no closer to our goals than when we started."*

"I know." Alistair replied. *"We have to tackle this in a completely different way."*

*

The ability to consistently make good decisions can be the key to getting what you want out of life. We all make countless decisions every day, and many of those decisions are made subconsciously. When you deliberately bring the process into the light of your higher-reasoning faculties, you can improve your skills at this vital part of life.

The biggest obstacles to mastering decision-making are harmful emotions (5.1). They can block us from learning to see reality for what it is, and from being radically open-minded. Painting an accurate picture of reality in your mind depends on two factors: **Navigating levels and synthesizing accurately.**

Synthesis means converting masses of data into a realistic picture of reality (5.2). We're bombarded by sense information all the time, so we need to find ways to separate the important information from the irrelevant information.

To accomplish this, the following methods can be used: Speaking to believable people, retaining a healthy skepticism, and understanding that things look bigger up close and in the moment than they do in hindsight.

Also, remember that everything is constantly in a state of flux. When you notice a change, either a positive or a negative one, you need to plot the rate of change over time. Slow, steady improvement is a good thing – but **it's not worthwhile if the projected improvement won't take you above the bar of excellence within an acceptable time limit (5.3).**

Understanding the way that **reality exists on different levels (5.4)** is one of the keys to effective synthesis.

Let's say you're still at school and your highest-level goal is to become an astronaut. On a slightly lower level, your goal will probably need to be to get a degree in science. On a different level, you need to have perfect health. On a still lower level, you need to get good grades at school, and on the lowest level, you need to study tonight instead of playing video games.

All the different levels interact with each other, and you interact with them. Most of us understand this intuitively, but **we often weight our decisions incorrectly because we're operating on or thinking about the wrong level.** A gut feeling can be useful, but it often takes only the lowest levels into account. It's better to rely on logic, reason, and common sense. In this way, you can visualize how your plans and intended outcomes will play out across multiple levels, and you will then be taking second- and third-order consequences into account too.

Think of every decision as a bet (5.5). Each bet has a probability of paying off, and a cost or a penalty if you're wrong. An **expected value calculation (5.6)** weighs the probabilities of being either right or wrong, multiplied by either the reward or the penalty, and subtracts one number from the other. Making a bet that carries a minimal risk and has a low chance of paying off may be better than a bet with minimal rewards but a high chance of success. It's worthwhile taking the time to work it out.

To decide effectively, you need to weigh your chances using the best logic and the best information you can get. Most choices have pros and cons – but few have no cons at all. The better you get at improving your odds when making important decisions, the more likely you are to succeed. Again, we know this intuitively, but we seldom put effort into doing the proper homework and researching it thoroughly. Usually, there's no time to deal with unimportant things – so **focus your time and energy on the "must-dos" instead (5.7).**

There are always going to be endless possibilities – but not all of those possibilities are equally probable. Practical thinkers know the difference between what's possible and what's likely to happen, and if they're not sure, they find out first.

In order to make good decisions more often than making bad ones, using these principles should become instinctive and habitual. **Simplify (5.8)** your choices down to the bare basics and slow down your thinking enough to be able to spot the recurring patterns ("another one of those").

Don't just accept opinions as facts. **Improve your decision-making by** carefully weighing the believability of **each opinion alongside the principles that are involved (5.9, 10).** Who you choose to listen to makes a big difference.

Over time, Ray Dalio and the staff of Bridgewater have used **systemized and computerized decision-making tools (5.11)** to great effect. Combining radical transparency with algorithmic decision-making has produced remarkable results.

Ray believes that Artificial Intelligence will play a big role in helping governments, companies, and individuals make better decisions in the near future.

Computers don't become anxious, they work 24/7, and they're completely objective. Combined with human intelligence and a **deep human understanding (5.12)** of the cause and effect relationships between things, they are wonderful tools. It's a brave new world, and in Dalio's view, we're better off being prepared to deal with it than wishing it simply wasn't true.

*

Lessons in Action: Application

When Alistair and Meg finally sat down together to talk about their future, they decided that whatever happened, they would work together as a team and agree on how to do it. As tough as it was to change, they both understood that something drastic needed to happen in their lives if they wanted to live up to their full potentials and get what they wanted out of their future.

"I bought a big notebook and some pens," Said Meg teasingly, "because I knew you wouldn't think of that!"

Alistair chuckled. "So how does this work? Come on – you're the one who read all the books!"

"We start by writing down our goals." She replied and wrote "BUILD OUR DREAM HOUSE" down on the first page.

"Wait," said Alistair, grabbing the pen and the notebook. "What about 'TRAVEL THE WORLD'?"

"Well, maybe we should think about ways to combine those two things. We've always thought that the best way was to build our home first and travel when we're older. Maybe there's another way. I've been reading Luke and Mindy's blog. Have you seen it? They're in Bali now."

"I thought Luke was still working for his dad, selling cars."

"No. They've both become digital nomads," Meg said. She pulled the laptop closer to show Alistair. "And they're loving it. Wouldn't that be something?"

After that first all-night conversation, some arguing, some crying, and some laughing, it became obvious to them both that there was still a lot they needed to know. But they agreed, at least, that they both wanted to travel and they wanted to buy a piece of land somewhere beautiful and peaceful. Once that idea crystalized, it was as if everything else began to fall into place.

Alistair began reading blogs about entrepreneurs and digital nomads who lived on the road and made money online. Meg discovered that there were opportunities to teach kids English in foreign countries. Over the next few months, they put together a plan and started working toward it steadily.

Each time they had to make a major decision, they sat down and talked it through. Each time the basis for making the decision was: "Does this get us closer to our goals?"

Then they imagined the future playing out in different ways, talking through all their options.

"If we start in Thailand..." Meg said pointing to an article she was reading, "Look here. Here's the cost of living, including rent, food, and travel." Alistair leaned over to look at what Meg was pointing at. "That way we can save at least $300 a month."

"You're really good at this!" He said, and started scribbling down the costs in their notebook.

Each time their emotions and their flighty personalities threatened to derail the plans, they went back to the basics, painful as it was, and figured out what to do next. Their final plan looked nothing like the original, but it was much better in many ways. They were learning to visualize the outcomes they wanted and figuring out how to deal with the obstacles that stood in their way.

Six months later, they boarded a plane and set off to Cambodia. There was much about their future that was still uncertain, but it didn't bother Alistair or Meg in the slightest. They were learning to make good decisions and the rewards were sure to flow from there.

"...it always pays to be radically open-minded and seek out believable others as you do your learning. Many people have emotional trouble doing this and block the learning that could help them make better decisions."

PART III:
WORK PRINCIPLES

"For any group or organization to function well, its work principles must be aligned with its members' life principles."

"Looping" to Success as an Organization

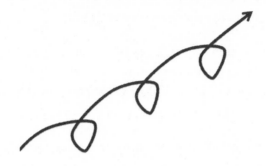

In *Principles*, Dalio explains his methodology regarding achieving success using the term "looping."

This means that when the inevitable problems occur that derail your intended pathway to success, you deal with each one in turn. **As you solve the first problem, you diagnose it and try to understand the root cause. That usually reveals a principle that will help you solve similar problems in the future.** You push the solution through, completing the first loop, and then continue on your upward trajectory. Then the next problem occurs, and you create another "loop" in the same way. The end result is a series of loops that continue upwards toward your intended goal.

The better you manage the process of looping, the quicker your trajectory ascends toward your goals.

When people in an organization feel that their personal values, the way they think, and what they want out of life are aligned to the goals, values, and culture of the organization, it's a recipe for an outstanding organization with a happy workforce.

The **people and the culture** are the two foundations upon which Bridgewater built its success for 40 years, and it was made possible by following the principles we have discussed so far.

Their company culture strives for excellence in all areas, and is solidly based on Dalio's hard-won life lessons. Each employee is encouraged to "act like an owner, responsible for operating in this way and for holding others accountable to operate in this way."

The following Work Principles show how the same ideas we've discussed are applied to the business world, and to larger organizations. This Work Principles section is further subdivided into three sections; the first is "To Get the Culture Right," the second is "To Get the People Right," and the third is "To Build and Evolve Your Machine."

"An organization is a machine consisting of two major parts: culture and people... Great cultures bring problems and disagreements to the surface and solve them well, and they love imagining and building great things that haven't been built before."

To Get the Culture Right

"You have to work in a culture that suits you. That's fundamental to your happiness and your effectiveness. You also must work in a culture that is effective in producing great outcomes, because if you don't, you won't get the psychic and material rewards that keep you motivated."

1: Trust in Radical Truth and Radical Transparency

Ray set out to build a real idea meritocracy, not just a theoretical one. For him, it was a system that brought together intelligent, independent thinkers and allowed them to productively disagree with each other. That resulted in the best possible collective thinking. It enabled the team to resolve their differences in a **believability-weighted way**. Their system has consistently outperformed every other decision-making system.

Dalio's definition: "**A pervasive Idea Meritocracy = Radical Truth + Radical Transparency + Believability-Weighted Decision Making.**"

In some companies, employees have two jobs. One is their real job and the other is trying to hold up the appearance of their job value to colleagues and superiors. Bridgewater finds this kind of approach awful, and more importantly, ineffective.

Instead, Bridgewater employees are encouraged to embrace the good, the bad, and the ugly about the truth. You only get stronger by doing difficult things. Not everyone has the integrity or willpower necessary to demand total transparency from others. Those employees that persist eventually find that they can't work in any other way.

The company culture creates an environment where everyone has the right to know, understand, think for themselves, and offer their honest thoughts without fear, and in a transparent way. This helps eliminate lies and injustice from the organization.

55

Total transparency is impossible. You can't share sensitive personal information when it would injure someone – but the idea is to push the limits of transparency and trust the process.

> *"For me, not telling people what's really going on so as to protect them from the worries of life is like letting your kids grow into adulthood believing in the Tooth Fairy or Santa Claus. While concealing the truth might make people happier in the short run, it won't make them smarter or more trusting in the long run."*

2: Cultivate Meaningful Work and Meaningful Relationships

Trust is one of the most valuable parts of a company culture to enforce and cultivate. It can only come from genuine relationships, not from forced ones. In the early days of Bridgewater, Ray treated his colleagues as an extended family, and it rippled out from there to include more and more people as the company grew.

Even in the best of companies, individuals who are harmful to the company's culture and goals will slip in. That's why it's vital to **be loyal to the common mission and objectives of the company rather than being loyal to those people who may go against it.**

Exceptional relationships rely on each member having a crystal clear idea regarding the value exchange. In other words, what is expected of them and what they can expect to receive in return? **People need to know where compromise is possible and where it is not possible.**

There's a difference between being fair and being generous. In order to be successful at instilling a transparent and trusting culture, you need to know where the line is in every situation and constantly stay on the side of fairness. People are people, and we know that **people lie to protect their own interests**. Avoid being naïve about it and treasure those capable few that operate with integrity even when you're not looking.

"Meaningful relationships are invaluable for building and sustaining a culture of excellence, because they create the trust and support that people need to push each other to do great things."

3: Create a Culture in Which It Is Okay to Make Mistakes and Unacceptable Not to Learn from Them

Successful people learn from their mistakes. Creating a culture of success means embracing the fact that mistakes are natural and that failing well and learning from the failure are better than hiding your mistakes.

Mistakes are painful, but shielding yourself or others from that pain is not the same as being kind or compassionate. Being frank and open about what went wrong and why it happened is the best way to **learn to love your mistakes**.

The fear of being wrong, and the fear of being found out, creates a terrible working environment that's filled with backbiting, lies, and malevolent barbs. When it's all out in the open, people tend to become even-minded, open, and more effective at their jobs. There's no point in feeling bad about your mistakes and shortsightedly focusing on the short-term outcomes. **It's better to accept failure and look at how that failure can guide your future evolution.**

When you understand that **nobody can see themselves objectively** and that everyone has blind spots, you can see the value of honest feedback. Dishonesty and ego-games can only get in the way of success.

Bridgewater keeps an **"issue log,"** which is a record of each and every mistake that was made along the way. By studying those mistakes and observing the patterns, they could determine which ones were the product of weaknesses and **where those weaknesses came from**. People were allowed to make mistakes, but it was unacceptable to make the same mistake twice.

"By creating an environment in which it is okay to safely make mistakes so that people can learn from them, you'll see rapid progress and fewer significant mistakes. This is especially true in organizations where creativity and independent thinking are important, as success will inevitably require the acceptance of failure as a part of the process."

4: Get and Stay in Sync

People work well together when they are aligned on many levels. Of course, this doesn't mean that conflict disappears. But the way these conflicts are handled is what matters. There's no point in getting mired in angry disputes or endless discussions – you need to follow a system based on clear principles.

In this chapter, Ray shares examples from Bridgewater in which subordinates openly challenged senior team members (himself included) **in both an open-minded and assertive way**. When certain disagreements created an impasse, they were raised to the Management Committee. At that point, the case was sent to the entire company by email so everyone could judge for themselves who was right and who was wrong.

The idea behind this revolutionary way of handling conflict was to **align everyone to the same principles** and to make a decision based on merits, not based on rank or autocracy.

To make it work in practical business situations, everyone involved needs to remain **calm and respectful** of the process. People need to learn to **get in sync with each other** and how to disagree well. It's an art, and it takes practice.

Naturally, there will always be those who remain closed-minded and those who argue simply for the sake of arguing. It pays to know who those people are, and if they can't work along with the team, they need to be removed. The person running the meeting needs to run the conversation and needs to be clear about the objectives, the levels of discussion, and the kind of disagreements that will help the process, not hinder it.

> *"...Alignment can never be taken for granted because people are wired so differently. We all see ourselves and the world in our own unique ways, so deciding what's true and what to do about it takes constant work."*

5: Believability Weight Your Decision Making

It makes logical sense to weigh more heavily the opinions of people who are more credible or who deal with the same or similar issue at hand than the opinions of those who don't. To make sure this happens, there needs to be fixed criteria for finding out who is most **believable**.

Bridgewater actually uses an app called the Dot Collector to manage this process. Combined with the baseball cards, each employee's input is tracked, and when it comes to voting, the system calculates not only the vote count, but a believability-weighted score too. A more believable person has two qualities. First, they have repeatedly accomplished the task at hand triumphantly. And second, they can succinctly explain the "cause-effect" relationship of their conclusions. When the vote count and the believability align, the decision is made and the team moves on.

The merits of an idea should always trump its popularity. That's where simple votes can let you down, whereas recognizing the real merit of each person's idea can succeed. It's important to focus on the **reasoning** behind the idea, rather than just the conclusions.

Simply letting everyone offer their opinions and randomly disagree with each other is a waste of time. Everyone has an opinion, but sometimes you have to assume the role of the teacher, and sometimes you have to be the student. You need to be humble enough to know which role is best for you in each situation. **The best** answers come from the best disagreements between the most relevant people.

At some point, the debate needs to end. Then you need to **let go of your need to be right** and decide in favor of the most effective solution using a fair system.

"...The best decisions are made by an idea meritocracy with believability-weighted decision making, in which the most capable people work through their disagreements with other capable people who have thought independently about what is true and what to do about it."

6: Recognize How to Get Beyond Disagreements

Life isn't always perfectly fair, and most disputes will end with at least one person being unsatisfied. Taking this into account, idea meritocracy needs to be **grounded on solid procedures** that allow you to get past hurt feelings and deadlocks. There needs to be a clear way to make the final decision.

Like the laws of the land, these principles can't be bypassed because two people agree to break the rules. If the principles you've agreed to are wrong, by all means, improve them – but make sure it's recorded and that everyone follows the same standards of behavior.

The right to take part in debate doesn't give everyone the equal right to make decisions. That must always remain the responsibility of one person who is accountable for his decisions.

If you leave important conflicts unresolved, there are bound to be consequences down the line; you will undo all the hard work you've already done and the system will backslide into anarchy. Everyone in the company needs to be onboard with the process, and once a decision is made, it should be accepted, even if individuals still disagree. **The cohesion of the group must supersede the feelings of the minority.**

To get the best out of Idea Meritocracy, someone has to have a **higher-level point of view**. From that vantage, you can see the merits behind each opinion but you're able to weigh up the believability of each one and assess the decision from a broader perspective.

"...a system [for settling disputes] is essential in an idea meritocracy, because you can't just encourage people to think independently and fight for what they believe is true. You also have to provide them with a way to get past their disagreements and move forward."

TO GET THE PEOPLE RIGHT

"A culture and its people are symbiotic—the culture attracts certain kinds of people and the people in turn either reinforce or evolve the culture based on their values and what they're like."

7: Remember That the WHO Is More Important than the WHAT

A business is like a machine, and the parts that make it work happen to be in the form of people. No matter how bulletproof your processes are, **if you have the wrong kind of person in the wrong job, there will be problems.**

Responsible Parties (like senior managers) bear the consequences of their decisions, so they must be capable of making tough calls and getting results at the highest levels.

It's only when 1) managers' **incentives are aligned with their responsibilities**, and; 2) when they **take full ownership** of their decisions that they will produce the best results. Companies don't make decisions; only people do that.

> *"When you know what you need in a person to do the job well and you know what the person you're putting into it is like, you can pretty well visualize how things will go."*

8: Hire Right, Because the Penalties for Hiring Wrong Are Huge

It's always tempting to hire people who are like you, but that doesn't always equate to the best possible hiring choice. A more sensible method is to **create a clear specification for the job** that needs to be done, and to match the candidates based on how they score **on values, abilities, and skills that suit the job**. Be scientific about it, and don't let your personal bias get in the way too much.

Not everyone sees things the way you do. When you are able to understand how you think and how other people think in different ways, your chances of finding the perfect fit will be much better. Never settle for an adequate fit. Instead, **search for the candidate who "sparkles."**

Remember, **people seldom change** on a fundamental level. You can teach someone, guide them, and encourage them, but they will always be the same kind of person at the core. If they lack character or are impractical idealists, there is little hope.

Choose someone who you want to share your life with – because essentially, that's what's going to happen. Don't be shy about sharing your "warts" or the things about your company that you'd rather hide; they'll find out soon enough anyway.

Pay north of fairly, and pay for the person, not the job. Offer incentives to keep your employees because it takes a long time to find the perfect match and it takes a lot of training and fine-tuning to reach optimum levels. Having to fire and rehire is never desirable.

"When you know what someone is like, you know what you can expect from them."

9: Constantly Train, Test, Evaluate, and Sort People

Exponential growth as a person can only come from development. **A business can only evolve and grow as quickly as the people who form the various parts of it are evolving and growing**. The two go hand in hand. To accomplish this, there needs to be open, frank, and sometimes painful conversations.

When you hire someone, you can never be sure about all of their strengths and weaknesses, and you can never accurately predict a person's career path. The Principles help you to remain open-minded, suspend your ego (as an employer or as an employee), and create enough room to make a few mistakes. How else can we grow? Book learning can only take you so far – the rest comes through **direct experience.**

Being too kind or feeling sorry for someone can only get in the way of the truth. Instead, the feedback that new employees get needs to be focused on accurate assessments of how well they are aligned to real goals and objectives. Most people overestimate their own importance, and few of them will appreciate that you're giving them the power to become successful through tough love.

Bridgewater managers are educated to "pay more attention to the swing than the shot." It's more important to **judge people on the way they think** and their reasoning abilities than only on isolated outcomes.

"When you get personal evolution right, the returns are exponential. As people get better and better, they are more able to think independently, probe, and help you refine your machine."

TO BUILD AND GROW YOUR MACHINE...

"Most people get caught up in the blizzard of things coming at them. In contrast, successful people get above the blizzard so they can see the causes and effects at play. This higher-level perspective allows them to see themselves and others objectively as a machine, to understand who can and cannot do what well, and how everyone can fit together in a way that will produce the best outcomes."

10: Manage as Someone Operating a Machine to Achieve a Goal

Your business is a machine that's designed to produce certain results. To diagnose and deal with problems, you need to be good at looking down on that machine from a macro perspective. From there, you can **study the machine like an engineer** and see whether or not the machine is moving you toward your goals.

Your metrics are your diagnostic tools, so they need to answer the most important questions and light the warning signals on your dashboard before it's too late to fix a problem. Whenever you solve another problem, **also think about how to improve your machine from what you've learned during the process.**

Dalio compares the way he manages people to being a ski instructor, which requires close contact with your students and spending time on the slopes through some trial and error. Soon enough, you can see what people can handle and what they can't. He gets his staff to write a brief report to him on a regular basis to keep his finger on the pulse. When he notices a "suspicious thread," he pulls it, so that small problems don't conflagrate into huge ones.

Your core Principles should be translated into the policies that hold your business together, and you need to consistently hold your people accountable to those without micromanaging them. At the same time, learn to appreciate them for holding you accountable too.

This way, you can keep evolving your machine, constantly improving your people and yourself.

> *"I built the machine that is Bridgewater by constantly comparing its actual outcomes to my mental map of the outcomes that it should be producing, and finding ways to improve it."*

11: Perceive and Don't Tolerate Problems

A healthy fear of being wrong means that you acknowledge your weaknesses, but you don't let the pain of dealing with them force you into accepting and tolerating those weaknesses, or worse, sweeping them under the rug. As Dalio says: " If you're not worried, you need to worry—and if you're worried, you don't need to worry."

It's easy to gradually slip from excellence towards mediocrity, especially when your business grows and more people join your ranks. **The head chef needs to keep "tasting the soup"** to make sure that standards are never allowed to slip.

Things don't just go wrong mysteriously. There's always someone specific doing something specific, so it is best to avoid generalizations and be courageous enough to fix the difficult things. If you can't fix them, you need to escalate, bring the problems out into the light, and get the best problem solvers to help you.

"Problems are like coal thrown into a locomotive engine because burning them up—inventing and implementing solutions for them—propels us forward. Every problem you find is an opportunity to improve your machine."

12: Diagnose Problems to Get at Their Root Causes

A common mistake businesses make is fixing problems without **properly investigating the root cause of the problem**. Doing so might alleviate the pain temporarily, but it robs you of a golden opportunity to tweak your machine and avoid similar problems in the future.

The best companies use principles like the 5-step process to pinpoint the underlying causes of constant errors and problems, enabling them to root out the problems for good. **They carefully analyze what core principles are involved**, and they don't confuse the approach that was taken with the circumstances themselves.

First ask yourself: Did my machine do what it was designed to do? If not, you need to find out why and fix the machine. Is it a once-off occurrence, or is there a pattern? Then figure out how your machine and your people need to evolve to the next level by asking yourself what a high quality person would have done in exactly the same circumstances with a perfect machine, and then keep asking "why?" – **Drill down into the deep specifics until the real root cause reveals itself.**

It's always tempting to rush through this process without being thorough and meticulous by the simple fact that other work is pressing and must be done. But if you understand that an **accurate diagnosis and quality planning are the foundations of creating a lean and effective machine**, you'll make the time.

"When you encounter problems, your objective is to specifically identify the root causes of those problems—the specific people or designs that caused them—and to see if these people or designs have a pattern of causing problems."

13: Design Improvements to Your Machine to Get Around Your Problems

Nobody can start from scratch and come up with a perfect recipe for a successful business. Bridgewater became successful, not because Ray Dalio knew all the answers when he started, but because he had the right attitude when facing painful mistakes and setbacks.

Each time they happened, he got better at designing and building his "machine." When his customer service wing began to slip and standards began to drop, he used this exact principle to fix the problem.

He took the most important principles and built them into habits by implementing them in practical, systematic ways with checks and balances to ensure the highest standards. He built his principles into algorithms. He trained people to see the principles at work in their day-to-day tasks. It took time and deliberate attention. It wasn't something that was just nice to have; it was essential.

Running the possible outcomes in his mind, as if they were movie scripts, **he learned to visualize who would do what and when, as well as the results those actions would produce.**

A well-designed machine takes into account the fact that people are not perfect. In Dalio's view, an organization is built from the top down, so he paid more than the usual attention to hiring the best top-tier people he could find. They, in turn, had to extend the pyramid downwards, designing their parts of the machine along the same principles. **This way, everyone in the organization reports to a believable person, someone who has the highest standards**.

Even so, **people are imperfect**, and you'll seldom find a person who has everything you want, so in some cases you need to design "guardrails." That might be in the form of another team member with complementary skills and strengths. It prevents people from making bad decisions because of their blind spots – and we all have our blind spots.

Finally, don't be naïve about dishonesty. Cheats are more common than you might think, so your procedures need to include investigations (in a transparent way) to make sure people are spending your money wisely, as if it were their own money.

"...For me, it's an almost visceral process of staring at problems and using the pain they cause me to stimulate my creative thinking."

14: Do What You Set Out to Do

Each of us has a different reason to get out of bed in the morning, and to work at what we do. It's easy to get lost in the task at hand and forget about *why* you love doing your job. To stay motivated, you need to **stay connected to your excitement, your passion, and to visualize the things you want to turn into realities.**

Transferring this enthusiasm to people who work for you isn't always easy. It's a challenge to stay in sync with team members and coordinate your reasons for achieving goals. Sometimes you have to use a carrot and sometimes it's a stick – but if you're not excited about what you're doing, then you should stop working for it.

Everyone has a lot to do, but those that get more done are used to calling on their creativity, their character, and their wisdom to achieve more. To quote Winston Churchill: "Success consists of going from failure to failure without loss of enthusiasm." In other words, **expect that problems will keep coming at you, so you can keep the right frame of mind about it**. Don't get frustrated, because failure is never final.

When the last item is ticked on the checklist, you can take some time to rest and restore balance – and **don't forget to celebrate your successes!**

"The organization, like the individual, has to push through to results in order to succeed—this is step five in the 5-Step Process."

15: Use Tools and Protocols to Shape How Work Is Done

It's easy enough to have good intentions – but those **good intentions on their own are not enough**. Behaviors only change when we cultivate new habits and those new habits takes practice.

Bridgewater went to great lengths to develop tools that embed Dalio's principles. These tools collect data on everyone in the company, no matter their rank, and the data is crunched in ways that everyone can challenge – to make the whole process transparent and fair. The principle of idea meritocracy could not function practically without these tools.

They've taken it a step further and what's **evolved is a system of internalized learning**. All of the meetings at Bridgewater are taped, and some are broadcast live or used as training materials, so team members can interact, vote, and offer suggestions from remote locations. Each one can be used as a case study for teaching and for aligning people to the company culture. Students input their own thoughts into the system and it tracks their strengths and weaknesses. In this way, Bridgewater can tailor their learning and their job assignments.

This fosters the kind of environment in which people feel valued and respected, and where they have the confidence to offer their insights and objections in an open-minded way. The principles are clearly stated, and anyone can track, assess, and challenge the logic behind almost every decision.

"Just as you can't learn many things by reading a book (how to ride a bike, speak a language, etc.), it's nearly impossible to change a behavior without practicing it."

16: And for Heaven's Sake, Don't Overlook Governance!

Governance means **implementing a system of checks and balances** into place that safeguards the organization from losing key staff members. **It also safeguards the values and principles** you've worked so hard to create, and it ensures that no single part of the machine is irreplaceable.

No single person should be more powerful than the system. Even teams and departments can splinter off into fiefdoms if there is nothing to prevent that from happening. When a single person is making all the decisions, there may be bottlenecks, and no single person is good at everything.

"[Governance] is the process that checks and balances power to assure that the principles and interests of the community as a whole are always placed above the interests and power of any individual or faction."

CONCLUSION

What you do with the Life and Work Principles we've discussed in this book is up to you. Ray Dalio's objective with this book is to inspire others to take these ideas even further, and to learn to struggle well in their own ways. Now that he has completed setting down his Principles for posterity, he is working on practical tools for people to use based on these ideas, and he plans to make them available soon.

His experiences led him to conclude that out of all the approaches to making winning decisions, an Idea Meritocracy is the best approach. Throughout his life, Ray has relished the process of forming meaningful relationships with great people. It has brought him deep satisfaction to evolve personally and crystalize his most important insights about life, business, and success into these Principles. The monetary success was just the icing on the cake.

There's no point in wishing that we lived in Utopia, and there's no such thing as perfect. However, there are great things, and it is possible to have a great life. To accomplish anything great, you need to put your honest thoughts out on the table, encourage thoughtful disagreements about those ideas with believable people, and work according to the principles that you believe are best.

As you go after the things you want, you'll be forced to make choices. Sometimes you'll succeed and sometimes you'll fail – and if you like, you can go with the flow, trusting in some higher power or destiny. If you want to struggle well, it's better to learn from the mistakes you've made without giving up on your goals or on yourself.

Make your work and your passion one and the same. Struggle well along with those whose mission is the same as yours, and savor those struggles as much as the rewards they bring.

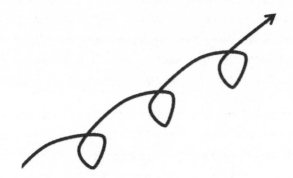

GIFT: GUIDED CHALLENGE

"Imagine that in order to have a great life you have to cross a dangerous jungle. You can stay safe where you are and have an ordinary life, or you can risk crossing the jungle to have a terrific life. How would you approach that choice? Take a moment to think about it because it is the sort of choice that, in one form or another, we all have to make."
– Ray Dalio

Now is the time to implement all that you have learned in this summary towards your life and professional goals! We know the overwhelming feeling of grappling with the new wealth of information you now carry... analyzing it, compartmentalizing it, and then applying it. To kill that tiny but overwhelming monster while it's small, we went ahead and formulated a **30-Day Guided Challenge to gradually ease you into massive action**. In the action plan, you will:

- Clearly complete a full cycle of goal setting and attainment using the 5-step process
- Develop a plan to become more introspective and personally identify your largest road-blocks to success
- Uncover your brain-type to understand who should surround yourself with to accomplish different objectives
- Take a top-down view of your team/business and identify any misalignments

Think of the **30-Day Guided Challenge as the last excuse on your shelf**. After reading the plan you simply have no excuses holding you back from implementing the insights of this book to your life.

Follow the steps below to instantly access your Guided Challenge:

1) **Open** your smart phone's camera application

2) **Aim** your phone's camera **and focus on** the QR Code below

3) **Click** the link that pops up on the top side of your screen

You can also download the 30-Day Guided Challenge by visiting the following link: **https://www.exegrowth.com/pdfguide-plw-37**

If you downloaded Power Insights at the start of the summary check your inbox, the Action Plan awaits you in a convenient and mobile-friendly PDF.

Our team at Executive**Growth** cannot thank you enough for believing in our work and trusting us to deliver the wisdom within *Principles* directly to you.

> *The mission of our team is to elevate the quality and productivity of our readers' personal and professional lives by providing clear, entertaining, and impactful summaries of timeless works.*

If you feel that we have done right by our mission, please leave a review on Amazon by visiting the following link **<http://bit.ly/egreview>**. Your review will sincerely go a long way for our growing company. You can also scan the QR code below to leave a review:

If you do not feel we met our mission or can improve we would love to hear from you too! We are always trying to make your experience better and your feedback is pivotal in the process – don't hold back any punches; we're pretty tough. Please leave your feedback by visiting the following link **<http://exegrowth.com/feedback>**.

We hold you in the highest regard for investing in yourself. We are committed to staying your companions in this exciting yet challenging journey of personal growth. **Let's go and let's grow!**

Links:

Principles **Full Book:** https://amzn.to/2A4UAyT
30-Day Action Plan: https://www.exegrowth.com/pdfguide-plw-37
Amazon Review: http://bit.ly/egreview
Executive**Growth Feedback:** http://exegrowth.com/feedback

Notes: Capture Your Thoughts

Made in the USA
Monee, IL
11 July 2020